# AT PEACE WITH MYSELF

## An Affirmations Workbook

# AT PEACE WITH MYSELF

## An Affirmations Workbook

**Linford Sweeney**

*Trafford rev. 08/08/2011*

 www.trafford.com

North America & international
toll-free: 1 888 232 4444 (USA & Canada)
phone: 250 383 6864 ♦ fax: 812 355 4082

~~~~~~~~~~~~~~~~~~~~

This book is dedicated to all my social networking "friends", who inspired me to write this book, and friends and family who believed in me even when I did not believe in myself.

Stay blessed.

~~~~~~~~~~~~~~~~~~~~

# CONTENTS

# PREFACE

I have been a Life Coach, trainer and mentor for the past ten years and always considered positive affirmations to be an essential element of the work that I did. This book came about as a result of my foray into social networking at the end of 2008. Whilst on these social networks I became aware that people needed some positive comments to help them through the week. Whenever I posted affirmations people were very approving and left positive comments on my status.

In time I created a Facebook group to address this need and begun sending weekly affirmations to individuals using social networking sites such as Facebook and Twitter, and to a more limited extent, by email. It was then that some people commented that I should publish a book of affirmations.

I have chosen to combine my Weekly Affirmations with life coaching especially aimed at people who may have been going through difficult or challenging situations in their lives, such as illnesses, redundancies, facing debt, raising teenagers, or daily battling the traffic to work that they may not like.

You can use these affirmations when you want to feel better about yourself by repeating them 7-10 times (out loud if you can), when it is safe to do so, each morning and evening.

Each affirmation contained within this book is designed to be repeated and meditated upon each week over a fifty-two week period. There is also the opportunity to keep a journal of your thoughts, lessons and any positive actions or achievements that may have come about as a result of using these weekly affirmations. Your journal as it develops may contribute to your own personal development and growth over the year.

# INTRODUCTION

## What Are Affirmations?

So, is there a definition for the word affirmation? One definition that I like says that it's "The act of affirming or the state of being affirmed" (English Collins Dictionary)

"Affirmations are positive statements that describe a desired situation, and which are repeated many times, in order to impress the subconscious mind and trigger it into positive action. In order to ensure the effectiveness of the affirmations, they have to be repeated with attention, conviction, interest and desire."

**"The Power of Affirmations" - Remez Sasson (www.successconsciousness.com)**

The use of positive affirmations is a technique designed to change the negative things we say about ourselves to something more positive. Although affirmations may not be an instant change, if you repeat it for 7-10 days, with honesty, trust, and belief, then results are most likely.

# Affirmations and You

It has been said that nearly 90% of our thoughts are negative. Most of us grow up learning to put ourselves down, believing certain things about ourselves, or comparing ourselves negatively to others. Affirmations were first spoken to you by your parents, then maybe your brothers and sisters, grandparents and many other family members. Later on there are likely to be your teachers, friends, and even people who you did not like. To tell you the truth you have been using affirmations yourself throughout your life. This is likely to continue until the end of your life.

Some of these affirmations were positive and others were negative. The negative affirmations that you may have heard throughout your life are unlikely to be true! Such affirmations may have put you down ("you'll never amount to anything"), or diminished your natural abilities ("you have two left feet"). However, not all negative affirmations heard during your lifetime have been deliberate. Many may have been said without malice or forethought. Yet they may have each had a negative effect on your life. How you chose to deal with what others have said to you has determined and shaped your character. The affirmations that you accepted and acted upon have determined your success and your ability to succeed.

You can choose to take control of your life and master your mind and your future with the use of positive affirmations. You will continue to say things to yourself about yourself for the rest of your life, and therefore it makes good sense to say encouraging, uplifting, inspirational and empowering words.

# About affirmations

* Affirmations are simple statements that we make, positive or negative.

* All our beliefs are stored in the subconscious mind.

* The subconscious mind is like your computer.

* Use the present tense. Hence don't say "I will be rich", but "I choose to be rich".

* Be positive. Only positive statements work.

* Affirmations can either be spoken or be written down.

* Daily repetition. Do them until you get your desired results.

* Successful people have used affirmations regularly.

# Will Affirmations help me?

Certainly! Whatever aspect of life you are dealing with, affirmations will help you to feel better about yourself and your life. Affirmations can manifest real change in your life. Removing the old negative self-limiting beliefs that may have been sabotaging you again and again throughout your life is crucial. It is an opportunity to achieve the life you have always wanted for yourself!

# Taking Stock – Your life right now!

Before you can undertake this journey in personal development and choosing to create new opportunities to make positive and real changes in your life, it is necessary to take stock about where you are in your life right now. The following questions are designed to help you to do this. These have been divided into the following categories:

• Personal/Spiritual Development
• Finance/Assets

- Physical Health
- Education/Career
- Work/Business
- Physical Environment
- Leisure Time Activities
- Friends/Family/Support Network

Example: current situation

| Categories | Current Situation |
|---|---|
| Personal and/or Spiritual Development | Meditate sometimes (once a week) Not really focused |
| Finance | Debts of £10,000 to repay Low income at the moment |
| Physical Health | Good, but need more regular exercise |
| Education and/or Career | Some qualifications in Social Care. |
| Work or Business | Full-time work in Social Care. |
| Physical Environment | Live in rented property in a poor area of town |
| Leisure Time Activities | Take holidays when I have the money |
| Friends/Family and/or Support Network | Single parent with two children Good friends and supportive family |

# Taking Stock of Your Current Situation
# (For you to complete)

It is important that the goals that you set yourself are: Specific, Measurable, Achievable, Realistic and Time-bound. Remember that although you want to touch the sky you have to be careful not to lose your footing. Keep your feet firmly on the ground.

| Categories | Current Situation |
|---|---|
| Personal and/or Spiritual Development | |
| Finance | |
| Physical Health | |
| Education and/or Career | |
| Work or Business | |
| Physical Environment | |
| Leisure Time Activities | |
| Friends/Family and/or Support Network | |

# What are your goals for the next twelve months?

The next step is to decide on your goals for the next twelve months. In other words, what you would like to achieve in the next twelve months. Set some goals that will take you there.

**Example: goals for the next 12 months**

| Categories | New Situation |
|---|---|
| Personal/Spiritual Development | Daily meditation for 10 minutes each morning and evening focusing on achievement of my goals |
| Finance/Assets | Create a debt management plan, including finding new sources of income and saving money |
| Physical Health | Establish a regime of regular exercise at the local leisure centre |
| Education/Career | Enquire about further qualifications in Social Care and enrol on a course that leads to a degree |
| Work/Business | Seek a better paid job in Social Care, maybe a promotion, or help to achieve further qualifications |
| Physical Environment | Set up a programme for moving to a less poorer area of town |
| Leisure Time Activities | Consider regular short breaks or one main holiday per year |
| Friends/Family and/ or Support Network | Maintain friends and family support |

# Setting New and Challenging Goals for Yourself.
## (For you to complete)

| Categories | New Situation |
|---|---|
| Personal and/ or Spiritual Development | |
| Finance | |
| Physical Health | |
| Education and/or Career | |
| Work or Business | |
| Physical Environment | |
| Leisure Time Activities | |
| Friends/Family and/or Support Network | |

# Peace

Peace surely comes from within.
That's where peace resides.
Within you and everyone else
Ready, but never taking sides

Be prepared to enter into
The vastness of your heart
To find the peace that surpasses
All understanding and thought.

Peace is not of this austere world
Nor any other sphere for that matter
Yet it transcends all things, and releases
A mind from incessant inner chatter

Real peace has no place in chaos,
Of outside circumstances, since
It is not dependent on such to be real
It delights in a call for patience

# SETTING PURPOSEFUL GOALS

# Week 1

## I Set My Goal

We don't always know what we want in life.

Maybe it's because we've never had it before. Or we've been told that we "can't" have it or we don't deserve it. It could be that others have told us that we're not capable. Or maybe we've just got fed up of trying and given up on our dreams.

Whatever you have experienced so far must be very frustrating for you.

However, from TODAY you can begin to develop a strong desire to achieve what you want. There must be a "burning desire" to achieve what you want ('Think and Grow Rich', Napoleon Hill).

You find that burning desire when you relax, focus on you, and concentrate on your goal. 'Feel it' within your body as part of your being.

### Affirmation

**"I am confident that once I set my goal, develop a strong desire to achieve it, and take positive action, then my success is assured."**

# Your Weekly Journal

# Week 2

# Despite My Fears

Sometimes we seem to think that because of fear its best to do nothing. However, doing nothing only continues to fuel that fear a little more each day. It's similar to leaving a forest-fire to continue to blaze and doing nothing about it. It is likely to spread.

It is by taking action that you diminish your fears. Action is the courage to deal with your fears and to build trust within. It could be as big as taking your first step to freedom.

Consider the stories of people who took action to make changes in their lives and the lives of others. For instance, Martin Luther King Jr, Rosa Parks, Sam Sharpe, Marcus Garvey, Gandhi, Nelson Mandela, or Emmeline Pankhurst. The list goes on.

You see, you are in good company!

### Affirmation

**"Despite my fears, I choose to take action.
Action diminishes all my fears."**

# Your Weekly Journal

# Week 3

# Getting What You Want

What do you really want out of life? Do you really know? At different times in the year people may begin to set goals, or try their best to keep to goals set earlier. Others set goals all the time. This could be your opportunity, if you haven't already, to set some goals for yourself. Decide what you want. Make sure that it's something that you feel passionate about. Then become determined to achieve it. Don't delay, begin right now.

## <u>Affirmation</u>

**"I choose to focus on what I really want and my passion and determination comes from my own self-belief and that of the greater power higher than myself."**

# Your Weekly Journal

---

# Week 4

# I Invest in Myself

It's not selfish to want the best for yourself, since as you grow and prosper you also influence, in a positive way, all the people that surround you. It is our growth that brings Love into the actions we take, puts Joy into our hearts, and Peace where before there was none.

There is no selfishness in what you do, just an understanding of the Spirit within you, and realising what is good and true. Fill your daily life with thankfulness and so satisfy your every need. When you know what you want and your words are positive and strong, you are able to say "I can" instead of "I can't".

Then you can drink from a fountain of abundance and feel joy growing within you, and peaceful assurance.

### <u>Affirmation</u>

**"Because I invest in myself, I am nourished with all that I need."**

# Your Weekly Journal

# Week 5

# Like-minded People

It has been said that you can tell a person's character by the company that s/he keeps. Your character is like your compass across the stormy seas of life. It protects you during the storm. It elevates you during the calm.

You choose your destination in life. You choose to pursue your dream, set your goals and establish milestones for success. Your character gets you there. Your destination is filled with other people on their various journeys.

There are also like-minded people along the way. Align yourself with these people and they can help you along the way. In the same way you too can help others.

### <u>Affirmation</u>

**"I choose to surround myself with like-minded people."**

# Your Weekly Journal

---

# Week 6

# Assured Success

Assuring your success can be crucial to your own sanity. However, you decide to define success, it's clear that everyone wants to have a successful life.

To do this there is a clear process to follow.

The first step is always to decide what it is you want to attract into your life. Without this first step it's much like preparing for a journey and not knowing where you intend to go.

### Affirmation

**"I am confident that once I know what I want, set my goals, and take action then my success is assured."**

# Your Weekly Journal

# STAY BLESSED

# Week 7

# Blessed in So Many Ways

Each of us is a blessing in the eyes of the Divine.

Each man/woman has worth and love distributed equally. The Divine never forsakes and take your pain lightly.

Consider the many other ways in which you and I are blessed. Write down your blessings.

It has been said that we should "count our blessings…one by one". Wise words indeed!

### <u>Affirmation</u>

**"Even in the midst of my pain I can always take comfort in knowing that I am blessed in so many ways."**

# Your Weekly Journal

# Week 8

## I'm blessed

Wherever my journey begins, I'm blessed.

When I awake each morning, I'm blessed.

Whatever I think about, I'm blessed.

Whatever I feel, I'm blessed.

Whoever I meet, I'm blessed.

Whatever I say, I'm blessed.

Whatever I do, I'm blessed.

Wherever I go, I'm blessed.

Whoever I think about, I'm blessed.

Whoever I am, I'm blessed.

Wherever my journey ends, I'm blessed.

I'm blessed.

### Affirmation

**"Wherever my journey begins, I'm blessed."**

# Your Weekly Journal

# Week 9

# Everything Happens for a Reason

When you begin to experience painful moments in your life, such as family bereavements, it is a time when you own vulnerabilities and immortality come into question.

I know that you and everyone else will experience these same feelings during our lives. However, we are all likely to deal with these situations in our own unique ways.

Death is inevitable, no matter how painful it is to you and me.

But life goes on!

### <u>Affirmation</u>

**"Even when things are not going the way I want them to go, I will simply trust that everything happens for a reason, and I will learn and grow from it all."**

# Your Weekly Journal

# Week 10

# My Inner Strength

The Divine created us with limitless resources. So who are we not to draw upon those inner resources to profit the world and to grow?

Each of us has phenomenal inner strength which can be accessed when we are aware of our own purpose for being in the world.

Remind yourself of your true purpose.

### Affirmation

**"I choose to develop my inner strength and recognize the limitless resources I have within me. I know I can do it."**

# Your Weekly Journal

# Week 11

# Feeling Good About Myself

Have you ever wondered why you are not attracting more good things and people into your life?

Each day, even when you try your best, you seem to feel more frustrated and unfulfilled than the day before. You continue to feel even worst about yourself. Then you begin to doubt yourself and your ability to change. You then start to attract even more negative feelings.

Does that seem familiar to you?

The truth is that you can attract all that you want into your life. One way is to begin to feel good about you. You do this by creating positive thoughts about your existing situation - whatever it may be.

### **Affirmation**

**"I deserve to feel good about myself and attract more good into my life. And I'm beginning right now."**

# Your Weekly Journal

# FINDING ACCEPTANCE

# Week 12

# Accepting Responsibility

It is sometimes difficult to accept responsibility for the things that we do.

Yet it is necessary.

We must each take responsibility for our actions. This can be difficult for some people because of past experiences.

A willing heart is a good place to begin. It's the first step to taking action.

### <u>Affirmation</u>

**"Accepting responsibility means being completely honest with myself about my mistakes and being willing to make positive changes."**

# Your Weekly Journal

# Week 13

# Accepting Me

Self-acceptance is crucial to your mental, physical and emotional health.

Accept yourself!

When you accept yourself you are affirming your humanity and your self-worth.

You are saying that you deserve to be in the world, deserve the best, and you have the right, as everyone else, to attract abundance, happiness and love into your life.

### <u>Affirmation</u>

**I choose to love and accept myself as I am – whatever life throws at me.**

# Your Weekly Journal

# Week 14

# Loving and Accepting Myself

It isn't easy to keep going when it seems like everything around you is falling apart.

You may believe then that taking the easy way out is the answer. For example: giving up.

And yet something inside you wants you to go on. Not to give up or give in to external pressures.

Know that when you truly love and accept who you are, then giving up or giving in is never an option.

### Affirmation

**"Even though I may feel like giving up or giving in, I fully and completely love and accept myself in every way."**

# Your Weekly Journal

# HEALING THE WHOLE PERSON

# Week 15

# Loving Myself

It is good to love yourself.

Self-love is essential to your mental, physical and spiritual health. Your self-confidence and self-esteem comes from self-love. Self-love will help you to look after your physical body.

Your spiritual needs are also satisfied through loving yourself, whether through a union with a higher power, through collective consciousness, or a commune with nature.

It is also said that you cannot love others without first loving yourself. Love is universal.

### Affirmation

**"Loving me heals all parts of my life. I choose to nourish my mind, body and soul."**

# Your Weekly Journal

# Week 16

# Every Cell in My Body

It has been said that our body obeys our every thought, whether positive or negative.

Thought is energy, and so is our physical body.

However, without Peace our thoughts and our bodies can have little rest or healthy expression. When Peace is your daily companion the expression becomes a positive one.

What more is there to be said for better energy and health?

### <u>Affirmation</u>

**"I have chosen Peace to be my companion this week; which means that every cell in my body vibrates with vital energy and health."**

# Your Weekly Journal

# Week 17

# Trusting the Healing Process

When ill-health and dis-ease takes hold of our bodies we sometimes give up without ever allowing the body to begin the self-healing process.

Self-healing has been tried and tested for as long as humans have inhabited the earth.

Together with modern medical support, trusting our own bodies is crucial to any healing.

### <u>Affirmation</u>

**"I trust the healing process within my body. I grow stronger and approve of myself in every way."**

# Your Weekly Journal

# LASTING THE JOURNEY

# Week 18

# I Am Thankful

Many people are living comfortably, whilst others are struggling to make ends meet. We can all recognize this situation around us.

Maybe we ourselves are in this self-same situation!

What is it that creates this gap? What about you? What are you doing wrong? What are you doing right?

How can you make things even better in your life?

This affirmation could help you to attract 'better' into your life:

### <u>Affirmation</u>

**"Because I am thankful for what I already have, I can attract into my life everything I desire."**

# Your Weekly Journal

# Week 19

## Getting Better and Better

Life can sometimes take a turn for the worse and we end up in a valley of despair.

A place where getting out seems like an impossible task. And yet for every valley there is a mountain.

Every day you stand in the valley looking up at that mountain.

One day your own courage, determination and clear focus will take you to the top of that mountain.

### <u>Affirmation</u>

**"Every day in every way my life is getting better and better."**

# Your Weekly Journal

_____

# Week 20

# Trust in the Process

Sometimes we need to let go and allow our Spirit to lead us. We need to realize that much happens in our lives to teach us important lessons about ourselves and the world around us.

For instance, that little argument that you had with someone may be teaching you forgiveness, patience, or love for yourself.

Or maybe that small disagreement with a friend is really an opportunity to learn important lessons about yourself so that you can add to your own knowledge and understanding. Thank your friend for the lesson.

Sometimes life just happens, and we need to be aware of this, and allow it to be so.

### **<u>Affirmation</u>**

**"I trust in the process of life, and therefore I am at peace."**

# Your Weekly Journal

# Week 21

# There is Time Enough

What have you been putting off doing for the past few days, weeks or even months? Another word for putting things off is called <u>procrastination</u>. It is where you put off until tomorrow what you could do today. It's always going to be done tomorrow, but that day never seems to come. It seems as if there isn't enough time in the day. Answer these five questions:

1  What's been stopping you doing this?
2  What, specifically, do you need to make this happen?
3  If you did it, would it contribute to your future goals?
4  Are you in control of what is needed to make this happen?
5  Can you do it right now, starting this minute?

Make some time right now. Just do it!

### <u>Affirmation</u>

**"I have all the time and resources to do everything that
I have planned, since there is abundance in my life and
I'm in control of my own destiny."**

# Your Weekly Journal

# Week 22

# Living in the Moment

I was recently reminded by someone about how important it is to remain in the moment.

Sometimes we tend to spend most of our lives in the past, for instance MOANING about what could have been. At other times we spend our time mostly thinking about the future, and WORRYING about what could be.

Moaning and worrying changes nothing! Instead we're more likely to live day-to-day in negativity and therefore hindering our progress, our chance to receive abundance that is available to all, and to creating fruitful and lasting relationships that can help us to grow and become better people.

Living in the moment means that you focus on "what is", and where you are now.

### **Affirmation**

"Today, I begin to see my true self, and discard the mistaken identities from the past."

# Your Weekly Journal

# Week 23

# Where I Am

Many times we beat ourselves up about what life has done to us.

Yet these life experiences, though seemingly painful and harsh, have made us who we are today.

Everything that you may have gone through in life can be used to create a better future.

In fact, it's essential! Have you too been tested in the fire of life?

### <u>Affirmation</u>

"Today, I am where I ought to be. Tomorrow is where I intend to be."

# Your Weekly Journal

# THERE IS ABUNDANCE

# Week 24

# Always Enough

The words this week are whatever you want them to be: a prayer, a mantra, or just a poem.

It's now clear that you choose the life you want for yourself.

It is also clear that a love that is real and divine can fill your heart with joy. It is joy that touches your very soul and can lead to your very own peace of mind.

It is s peace beyond all understanding that quietly and gently, and without judgment, leads your soul to truth.

### **Affirmation**

**"There is always enough love for me and for
everyone else around me."**

# Your Weekly Journal

---

# Week 25

# I Change Myself

Many people enter relationships with a desire to change their partner. Such changes have to be mutually acceptable. The problem arises where the change isn't mutual and acceptable by one partner, and this partner is then put under pressure to change.

This is likely to lead to frustration, anger, fear, inadequacy, low self-esteem, and resistance, or other negative emotions. This isn't likely to lead to a strong, vibrant, mutually acceptable and positive relationship. Instead, endeavour to change yourself.

By doing this you allow others to see your desire for personal growth, and your need for mutual acceptance.

### Affirmation

**I choose to be free from seeking to change other people,
but rather I change myself instead.**

# Your Weekly Journal

# Week 26

# I Grow

We all need to grow – physically, mentally and spiritually.

To do this we must first recognise and then develop our God-given abilities. To do this you need to have confidence. You therefore need to grow.

You do this by daily recognizing and realizing your own abilities.

We all have abilities. So write them down.
Do it now!

### **<u>Affirmation</u>**

**"Day by day confidence in my own abilities is growing. And I am now more able to accomplish my most desired goals."**

# Your Weekly Journal

# Week 27

# I Grow Stronger

Life is full of challenges, and with each challenge you may feel that you get weaker! However, each challenge may just be a test that is designed to make you stronger.

Strength comes from learning the lessons taught by each challenge, and putting those lessons into action. Growth comes from strength. You may go on to become a rock to others going through their own challenges. You are likely to experience many blessings.

In time, and through positive thoughts and determination, you may, if you have not already done so, find your life's purpose.

### <u>Affirmation</u>

**"Even though I am faced with so many challenges in my life right now, I choose to learn and grow stronger each day."**

# Your Weekly Journal

# REMAINING POSITIVE

# Week 28

# Always Able to Change

Change is inevitable.

It has been said that change and death are the only two certainties in life.

Some say that they are one and the same thing. But know that YOU are a part of that change process.

Don't allow yourself to be stagnant or remain where you are. Change will overtake you.

Whatever you may belief, feel, say or do, change is inevitable. There's nothing more to be said.

### **<u>Affirmation</u>**

**"I choose to be positive in all that I think about, in the knowledge that I am always able to change my life - no matter what else is going on around me".**

# Your Weekly Journal

# Week 29

# Yes I Can

Barack Obama said it well...YES WE CAN. Turn the 'WE' into 'I' and apply it to yourself. It is from the "I" that the "WE" begins to become an even more powerful force in all our lives. Together we are strong, but true strength begins within each of us.

When we join forces with another similar person, that strength is trebled! It is well-known in the business world as synergy - where one plus one equals three. A third force, most likely a divine intervention, joins us on our journey.

Togetherness brings Love, Joy and Peace. These are expressions of Divine Synergy.

### <u>Affirmation</u>

**"Even in the midst of strife, war, poverty and disillusionment,
I still hear the words "yes I can."**

# Your Weekly Journal

# Week 30

# I Allow Positive Thoughts

Many people spend their time thinking about negative things - worrying about what others may have said about them or thinking about what they don't want in life.

So what do you do instead? Firstly, make the decision to change your thinking. Choose to think positive thoughts. Dare to make changes in your life. Begin to love yourself.

Secondly, you need to release negative thoughts by replacing them with positive thoughts.

Thirdly, begin to feel good about yourself. Positive thoughts make you feel better about yourself.

### Affirmation

**"Today, I allow myself to think only positive thoughts, and choose to release negative thoughts and all that hinders my progress in life."**

# Your Weekly Journal

# Week 31

# Choose to be Positive

Your thoughts are powerful. Change your thinking, change your life. Bring your cherished goals and dreams closer to reality.

To do this you need to be positive in your approach in all circumstances.

Be positive in your thoughts and positive words and deeds will surely follow.

### <u>Affirmation</u>

**"I choose to be positive in all that I think about, in the knowledge that I am always able to change my life - no matter what else is going on around me."**

# Your Weekly Journal

# BUILDING YOUR INNER STRENGTH

# Week 32

## I Choose to be Strong

On some days it's difficult for us to focus on what we need to do.

Our usual response is to give in to our weaker self, become negative and lose confidence in our ability to change the situation to our advantage.

When we do decide to make the necessary changes it also changes our emotions. Some people call this The Feel Good Factor.

When you feel good about yourself it is very difficult to be anything but strong, positive and self-confident.

### Affirmation

**"I choose to present a strong, positive and self-confident image of myself today."**

# Your Weekly Journal

# Week 33

## It Is So!

What you think about each minute of each day determines the results you receive at the end of that day. So you think carefully.

The words you use each time you speak has an impact, not just on you, but everyone else around you. So you speak carefully.

Your actions, whatever they maybe and however they come about, will impact your day, your week, your month, your year, and your lifetime. So you act carefully.

It is so!

### <u>Affirmation</u>

**"I choose to see myself as strong, confident and capable.
And it is so."**

# Your Weekly Journal

# Week 34

# I Face New Challenges

We all face challenges in our lives. It's how we learn about ourselves, other people and the world around us.

Life, it seems to us, may be more difficult for some than others. It's not necessary to dissect other people's lives but rather to understand your own.

Where there have been successes and achievements in your past actions then remember these always when you face new challenges.

### <u>Affirmation</u>

**"When I'm faced with a new challenge, I look to past successes to boost my confidence."**

# Your Weekly Journal

# Week 35

# I Remain in the Present

Seek to focus upon living more and more in the present.

Stay in the NOW!

Find a quiet place to sit down and concentrate on your breathing. Be aware or each breath, as you inhale and exhale. Soon you will also be aware of feeling and listening to your heartbeat! In that moment you are in tune with yourself, and the true harmony of the universe.

The only real moment is now - the past is gone and never to be repeated, and the future is yet to come.

Fill your mind with true and pure LOVE. Allow that love to permeate your whole body. Do this each day.

Create space for harmony in your life.

### Affirmation

**"I choose to make time for me, and to remain in the present so that I can focus on love."**

# Your Weekly Journal

# ASKING FOR FORGIVENESS

# Week 36

# Forgiveness

To feel free and released from the past, we must forgive.

It is essential that we forgive others – and ourselves too! Until we can overcome our natural and very human feelings of fear, resentment, anger and guilt - justified or not - these emotions are likely to damage your ability to get on with your life.

Something can be done. And it can be done now, today, in this moment.

Acceptance of your emotions is a great start. Then be prepared to let them go.

### <u>Affirmation</u>

**"It is not the events, but how I respond to them, that define the joy, peace and happiness in my life."**

# Your Weekly Journal

# Week 37

# My Forgiving Heart

People sometimes wonder why they have no love in their lives. It usually seems to be the fault of someone else. They make excuses for their plight whenever they can.

Others may wonder when these people are going to start living.

An attitude of forgiveness is one way to begin to address the issue.

### Affirmation

**"I am thankful for my forgiving heart, and I am now ready for love to appear in my life. I am becoming a better person day by day."**

# Your Weekly Journal

# SO MUCH JOY

# Week 38

# It Is Okay

Sometimes you may think that other people should be having all the fun and enjoyment in life.

You may think that fun isn't for you; or you feel guilty whenever you think about doing it for yourself. Maybe something happened in the past to make you think that way today.

Could it be that you don't love yourself anymore?

Whatever it is, you can change the way that you're thinking right now. Decide to have some fun and enjoy yourself. As long as you have breath, then nothing can stop you.

Just do it!

### <u>Affirmation</u>

**"It is okay for me to have some fun and enjoy my life. And I do."**

# Your Weekly Journal

---

# Week 39

# I Share My Happiness

There are likely to be many 'good days' in your life where you are able to relax, consider your life's desires, and probably commune with nature.

Sometimes we're so cluttered with negativity and the 'bad days' that these wonderful times can pass us by.

Recognize the good days and allow the happiness within you to warm your heart, if just for a moment, and in so doing you'll be able to share those days with others.

### <u>Affirmation</u>

**"When my life is going well I choose to share my happiness with all those around me."**

# Your Weekly Journal

# Week 40

# At Peace with Myself

Peace comes from a Divine place. When you find that place you have tapped into the Creative Force that manifested life and all that there is.

You are a part of all that there is…and all that there could be.

From this place you are likely to experience many changes. Those changes could begin today. Start by looking within yourself.

Awaken the Divine Spirit within yourself.

### <u>Affirmation</u>

**"I am at peace with myself and comfortable in every area of my life. I am strong and capable."**

# Your Weekly Journal

# Week 41

# Feeling Wonderful

When was the last time that you could say that you felt wonderful?

It's clear that feeling wonderful about yourself can affect your whole demeanour and your outlook on life.

Each of us is created unique and wonderful in the eyes of the Divine.

Who are we to consider ourselves any less than the Divine's vision for our lives?

Louis Armstrong sung "Wonderful World" and said it all.

### Affirmation

**"Today is my day to feel wonderful. And all is well in my life."**

# Your Weekly Journal

# Week 42

# Feeling the Passion

We can all manifest our dreams – if we follow the age-old formula.

Are you thankful for what you already have in your life? For example, health, family, work, a roof over your head, good friends, food on the table, or clothes on your back.

Maybe you already have all of these. Now decide what else you want in your life – and it doesn't have to be material things.

Then visualize it as already happening. Use affirmations to bring it to fruition. Then just be patient. That's the formula.

### <u>Affirmation</u>

**"When I feel passionate about something I want, and
I visualize it daily, I am confident it will appear in my life."**

# Your Weekly Journal

# IT'S ALL ABOUT LOVE

# Week 43

# I Deserve Love

Many people believe that no love is in their lives. That is always so sad.

The Divine laws of the universe provide love in abundance - enough for everyone. We don't need to buy love, it's given. It's free!

Allow love to enter your heart and wash away the doubts and past despair that currently abide there.

You cannot continue to miss out on so many great gifts that are waiting to adorn your life. You can start right now.

### <u>Affirmation</u>

**"I know that I deserve love and readily accept it into my life - starting right now."**

# Your Weekly Journal

# Week 44

# I Am Love

Love guides our lives. It's an emotion that we can never live without.

What would a world without love look like? We dare to think about it. Instead we continue to develop love for ourselves, and in so doing we have more love to give to others.

However, love is much more than an emotion. Many believe that love has been with us since the creation of the world - and maybe before that.

Love is said to be of spiritual origins and therefore much older than our more recent emergence in the world in human form. It has been said that we are spirits having a human experience.

### Affirmation

**"I am love. As I share love with others,
every day I become stronger."**

# Your Weekly Journal

# Week 45

# Love embraces me

Sometimes, with so many people around you, you still feel unloved. It seems as if the whole world is going about its business and has left you behind. You feel as if you have no-one to call or visit or turn to when you're feeling low. What can you do?

Love is the answer! Love is the key that can open up the door to your heart. There is always enough love to go around. You need your share of that love too. It's around you – all the time! It's always there: the keeper of your heart. And it's free!

Take time out to be still. Ask that love enter your heart once more. Pray, reflect or meditate. Listen for love. You will know when it's there. When you do this love will always find you, embrace you, and comfort you.

You will then seek to share your love with others. Love will always attract love.

### <u>Affirmation</u>

**"I know that for me to connect with love I need to be still, ask and listen. When I do this every day, love embraces me. And I embrace love."**

# Your Weekly Journal

# Week 46

# Worth Loving

It is essential that you re-affirm your self-worth, the God-given gift that adorns your soul, caresses your spirit, and hugs your heart in truth and love.

People seem to put so little value on their own worthiness.

Our self-worth has always been with us, and it's always there – wherever we are. It is what makes us real, sincere and complete.

Re-affirm your own worth. You don't always need external validation.

### <u>Affirmation</u>

**"I am worth loving. Even with all my imperfections. I am a wonderful miracle of life."**

# Your Weekly Journal

# Week 47

# Good Enough

Many times we forget to say THANK YOU!

Make it a daily prayer to say thank you for what you already have, and what you are about to receive. And it is quite a simple process, though few of us find it easy. The question is not why we find it difficult to say thank you, but more about how we can make it more accessible and easier for those people who may need to say it most. One simple answer is to say 'thank you' for everything as you go through your daily activities. That way you don't miss anything!

Thankfulness today...many special gifts tomorrow!

### <u>Affirmation</u>

**"I am so very thankful for what I have today, because I know that my best is always good enough."**

# Your Weekly Journal

# Week 48

# Loving Myself

Recently, I've been talking with so many people who are experiencing health challenges.

Many believe that it doesn't have to be that way. It seems that we have all the necessary processes within our bodies to fight off dis-ease. It has been shown that it could be down to our thinking process. Yes, it is quite clear to many people today that what we think about most is likely to become our reality.

Positive affirmations may contribute to the healing process.

### <u>Affirmation</u>

**"Loving myself simply means that every cell in my body vibrates with energy and health."**

# Your Weekly Journal

# AT PEACE WITH MYSELF

# Week 49

# A Spirit of Peace

Sometimes you may feel as if my world is falling apart around you. Or the whole world is against you.

There seems to be no escape from negative people, the work you dislike, the partner that abuses you, the ill-health that follows you everywhere you go, or the dependency that threatens to take your life.

However, through it all there has to be hope - a knowing that all will be well. You sometimes feel peace within, if only for a short time, whenever you look within.

So you always try to find some ME time. You meditate, or just relax for awhile, away from all interruptions, so as to find that peace.

Then you're safe.

### <u>Affirmation</u>

**"I know that when everything else seems to be falling apart in my life, there is a Spirit of Peace within that always seeks to protect me."**

# Your Weekly Journal

# Week 50

## True to Myself

"Be honest with yourself".

You may have heard that phrase used before. How many of us are honest with ourselves? Sometimes, subconsciously, we say one thing and yet do the exact opposite.

In this case we may listen to both our head and heart and get different answers. Here we can bring both together by taking time out to think about things and recognizing how we feel about them.

We need to take time out to be true to ourselves.

### Affirmation

**"Every day in every way I am becoming more and more true to myself."**

# Your Weekly Journal

# Week 51

# A Self-confident Image

On some days it's difficult for us to focus on what we need to do. Our usual response is to give in to our weaker self, become negative and lose confidence in our ability to change the situation to our advantage.

When we do decide to make the necessary changes it also changes our emotions. We choose to be more than what our situations impose upon us. And we feel better for that. Some people call it "The Feel Good Factor".

When you feel good about yourself it is very difficult to be anything other than strong, positive and self-confident.

### <u>Affirmation</u>

**"I choose to present a strong, positive and self-confident image of myself today."**

# Your Weekly Journal

# Week 52

# Self-image

The way that you are seen by others can drastically affect your life. But first you need to find out how you see yourself.

You require a self-image that will, make you feel good about you, tell people who you are and at the same time help you to attain your stated goals in life.

For this you will need self-confidence as a first step.

### Affirmation

**"I choose to portray a strong, positive and self-confident image of myself."**

# Your Weekly Journal

# Peace Reigns

Where peace reigns
nothing else remains
but love and understanding,
and faithful joy outstanding.

In your breath lies
a Spirit that defies
what's impossible,
and hosts the improbable.

~ Linford Sweeney

# Your Personal Growth

For those people who have, through patience, perseverance and determination, managed to work through all fifty-two affirmations – well done! If you have not been able to do that so far that's okay too. Your own desire for self-growth will eventually take you through to the end.

If you are reading this without having gone through the weekly affirmations, then I suggest that you do and then return to this page later. To get the best from this book you will need to experience each affirmation (or as many as apply to you) for yourself. Only then are you able to realize your own personal development.

The following questions will help you to reflect on your own growth during the past fifty-two weeks. It is hoped that by now you would be ready to continue your journey of self-discovery and ready to take your learning to the next level. Use the following questions to help you to do this.

## What are your thoughts about this journey that you embarked upon fifty-two weeks ago?

# Over the past year what have you learned about yourself that you never knew before?

# Have you already put into practice what you have learned?

~~~~~~~~~~~~~~~~~~

**What other actions (not already mentioned above) have you taken to make real and lasting changes in your life?**

## What have you actually achieved during your affirmation journey?

~~~~~~~~~~~~~~~~~~~

**Since personal development is an ongoing journey, what are your plans for the coming 52 weeks?**

# Your Achievements Over the
# Past 12 Months

| Categories | Current Situation |
|---|---|
| Personal and/or Spiritual Development | |
| Finance | |
| Physical Health | |
| Education and/or Career | |
| Work or Business | |
| Physical Environment | |
| Leisure Time Activities | |
| Friends/Family and/or Support Network | |

# Setting New and Challenging Goals for the Next 12 Months

Goal-setting is an essential process along the journey of life. Each success takes you a little further to your ultimate goal through the learning of new lessons and the process of Continuous Growth

| Categories | New Goals to be established |
|---|---|
| Personal and/ or Spiritual Development | |
| Finance | |
| Physical Health | |
| Education and/or Career | |
| Work or Business | |
| Physical Environment | |
| Leisure Time Activities | |
| Friends/Family and/or Support Network | |

# How to use affirmations

Affirmations can be repeated anywhere. However, it is important to choose a safe place to carry out your affirmations, since your total focus may affect other activities that you may be undertaking at the time. For example, some people repeat their affirmations with their eyes closed so as to increase concentration.

Repeat them always, in a quiet place, in sessions of 5-10 minutes each, several times a day.

Relax any physical, emotional or mental tension while affirming. This is likely to focus your mind and the feelings you put into the act. Results come quicker this way.

Choose only positive words describing what you really want. Choose words that evoke positive images in the mind.

The power of affirmations can help you to transform and attract what is best for you into your life.

## Some useful techniques

**Mirror Technique:** This technique is great for helping you see yourself as beautiful.

**Anywhere technique:** This is used whenever you catch yourself thinking something you would rather not.

**Writing Technique:** Simply sit down at a table and write what you would like in your life 15 times every day.

**Trash Can Technique:** Good for getting rid of negative thoughts.

**Meditation Technique:** Look for divine inspiration while repeating your affirmation.

**Exercise Technique:** Very nice for active people and for many health related goals.

**Integration Technique:** A technique for actively working on your goals

# WORKSHOPS

A series of workshops designed to help participants to set effective and positive affirmations and to show how they can be best used as part of an overall personal development programme or lifestyle will run alongside this book.

These workshops will follow a tried and tested personal development model developed in Manchester between 2007 and 2010. This model takes from Life Coaching, NLP and Stress Management and uses experiential methods covering topics such as belief change, the law of attraction, outcomes setting, visualization and guided imagery.

For further information about these workshops you will need to regularly check the following website for dates and venues. The website address is www.peacefulconsciousness.com

# Useful Quotations

"As a man thinks in his heart, so he is"
~ The Bible

"We become what we think about"
~ Earl Nightingale

"...our life is what our thoughts make it."
~ Marcus Aurelius

"They can because they think they can."
~ Vergil

"A man is what he thinks about all day."
~ Emerson

"You are what you think about all day long."
~ Dr. Robert Schuller

# BIBLIOGRAPHY

"You Can Heal Your Life", Louise H. Hay

"Think and Grow Rich", Napoleon Hill

Vital Affirmations
www.vitalaffirmations.com/affirmations.htm

Affirmations for Radical Success
www.affirmations-for-radical-success.com/what-are-affirmations.html

Self-help and Self-development
www.self-help-and-self-development.com/affirmations.html

Gems 4 Friends
www.gems4friends.com/affirmations.html

Success Consciousness
www.successconsciousness.com

# Staying in Touch

The author would like to thank everyone who has purchased or used this book for the own self-discovery. He would be happy to take enquiries and receive comments about the book and stories about people's progress.

He may be contacted via his website which is
www.peacefulconsciousness.com